Explore OCEAN HABITATS with Elmo

Charlotte Reed

Lerner Publications ◆ Minneapolis

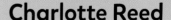

There are many habitats to explore!

In the Sesame Street® Habitats series, young readers will take a tour of eight habitats. Join your friends from *Sesame Street* as they learn about these different habitats where animals live, sleep, and find food and water.

Sincerely,
The Editors at Sesame Workshop

Table of Contents

WHAT IS A HABITAT?

Let's explore habitats! A habitat is a place where animals live and can find water, food, and a place to sleep. The ocean is a type of habitat.

Elmo loves learning about the ocean!

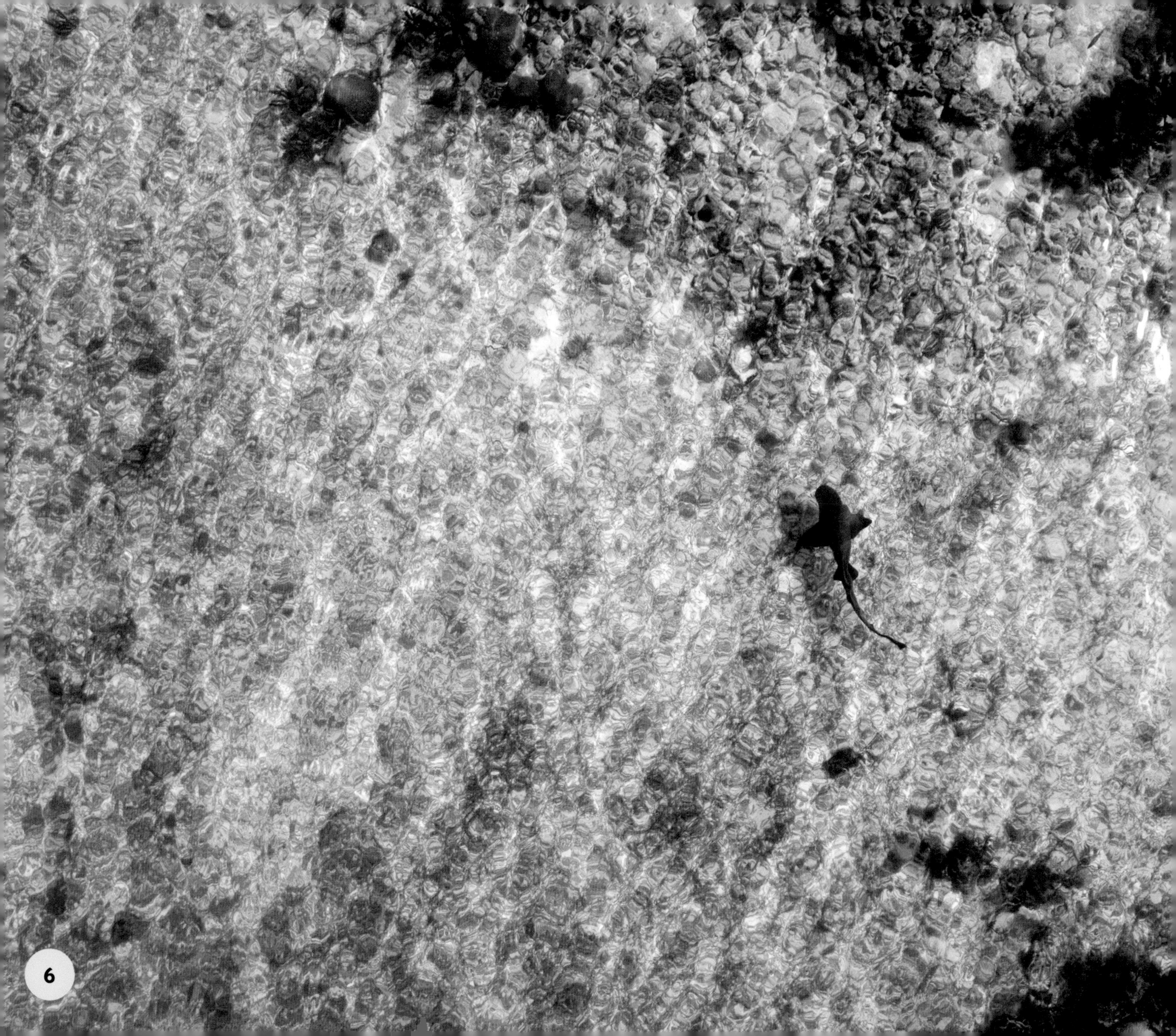

Oceans are large areas of water. There are five oceans in the world. They are the Antarctic, Arctic, Atlantic, Indian, and Pacific.

I went to the beach with Granny Bird and saw the Atlantic Ocean.

LET'S LOOK AT OCEAN HABITATS

The ocean is so big! Some ocean animals and plants are still being discovered.

I can't wait to explore the ocean. There's a clownfish!

Many kinds of fish live in the ocean! Some of the world's smallest animals live in the ocean too. A group of fish is called a school.

Look at all those fish!
There are so many for
me to count!

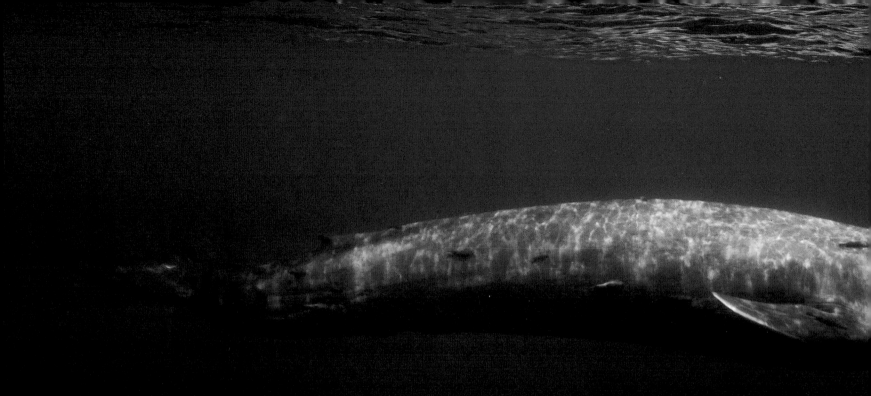

Large animals also live in the ocean. The largest
animal in the world is the blue whale. It is as
long as three school buses and can be found in
almost every ocean.

13

Kelp forests grow in the ocean. These underwater forests provide food and shelter for fish and other ocean animals.

Kelp needs plenty of sunlight to grow!

Sea otters make their homes in kelp forests. They also float along the top of the water to nap and eat food.

Sea turtles live in the ocean too. They sometimes swim near the ocean's surface. They poke their heads out of the water to breathe air.

Sea turtles have flippers that help them swim in the water.

Some ocean animals live closer to the bottom of the ocean. This stingray covers itself in sand on the ocean floor to eat and rest.

Some stingrays swim by flapping their fins like wings!

Coral reefs are found in oceans. Coral looks like colorful rocks. Coral reefs have been around for a very long time.

23

Seahorses live in coral reefs. When a seahorse eats or rests, it wraps its tail around coral or another plant.

Baby seahorses are called fry!

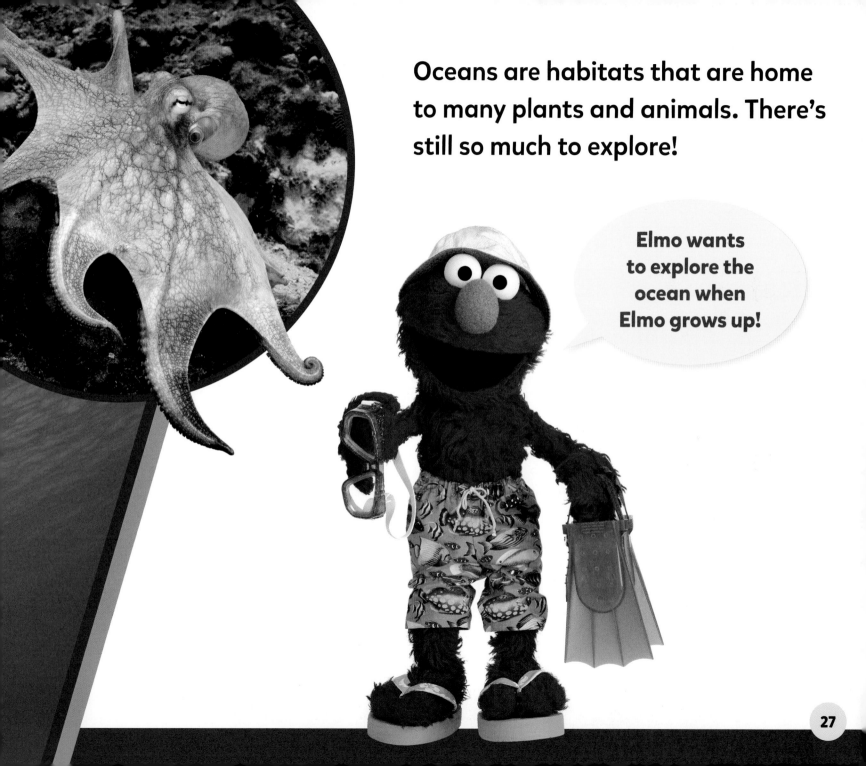

Oceans are habitats that are home to many plants and animals. There's still so much to explore!

Elmo wants to explore the ocean when Elmo grows up!

CAN YOU GUESS?

1. Which picture is of an ocean habitat?

A

B

2. Which of these animals lives in an ocean habitat?

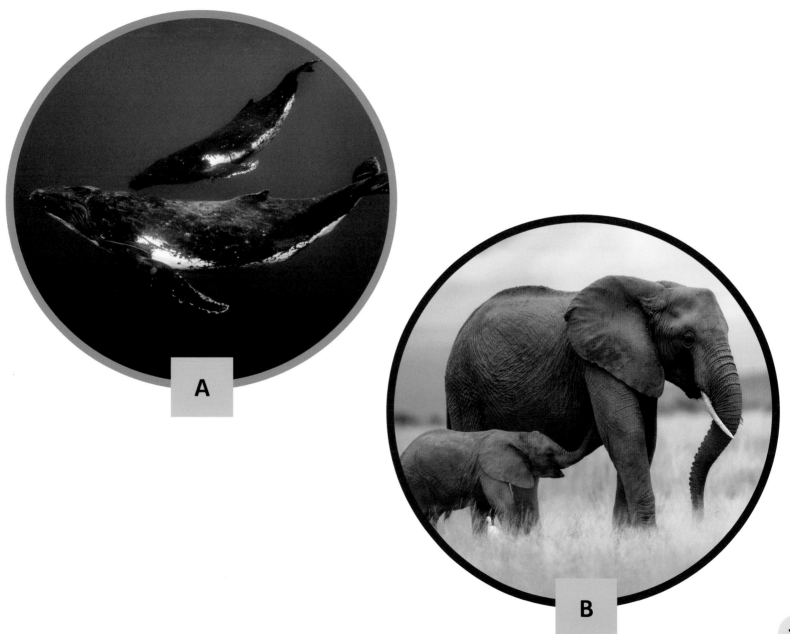

A

B

Glossary

flippers: flat limbs an ocean animal uses for swimming

habitat: a place where animals live and can find water, food, and a place to sleep

shelter: a place that covers or protects animals

surface: the upper parts of an area of land or water

Can You Guess? Answers

1. B
2. A

Read More

Culliford, Amy. *Super Cute Ocean Animals*. New York: Crabtree, 2023.

Reed, Charlotte. *Explore Freshwater Habitats with Gabrielle*. Minneapolis: Lerner Publications, 2024.

Sabelko, Rebecca. *Ocean Animals*. Minneapolis: Bellwether Media, 2023.

Photo Acknowledgments

Image credits: IakovKalinin/Getty Images, p. 5; Wirestock/Getty Images, p. 6; bugking88/Getty Images, p. 9; Georgette Douwma/Getty Images, p.10; eco2drew/Getty Images, p. 12; fdastudillo/Getty Images, p. 15; net_fabrix/Getty Images, p. 16; M Swiet Productions/Getty Images, p. 18; Gerard Soury/Getty Images, p. 21; mihtiander/Getty Images, p. 22; GOLFX/Getty Images, p. 25; Kurit afshen/Shutterstock, p. 26 (clown fish); NaluPhoto/Getty Images, p. 26 (dolphins); Humberto Ramirez/Getty Images, p.27; fhm/Getty Images, p. 28 (left); Damocean/Getty Images, p. 28 (right); Philip Thurston/Getty Images, p. 29 (whales); Vicki Jauron/Babylon and Beyond Photography/Getty Images, p. 29 (elephants).

Cover: Gerard Soury/Getty Images (anemone); lingqi xie/Getty Images (Qinghai Lake); Paul Souders/Getty Images (stingray); M Swiet Productions/Getty Images (turtles).

Index

For the mentors who helped me become smarter, stronger, and kinder: Bridget, Jennifer, Karen, Meg, and Sue

Lerner Publications Company
An imprint of Lerner Publishing Group, Inc.
241 First Avenue North
Minneapolis, MN 55401 USA

For reading levels and more information, look up this title at www.lernerbooks.com.

Main body text set in Mikado provided by HVD.

Designer: Laura Otto Rinne
Lerner team: Martha Kranes

Library of Congress Cataloging-in-Publication Data

Names: Reed, Charlotte, 1997– author.
Title: Explore ocean habitats with elmo / Charlotte Reed.
Description: Minneapolis : Lerner Publications, [2024] | Series: Sesame Street habitats | Includes bibliographical references and index. | Audience: Ages 4–8 | Audience: Grades K–1 | Summary: "The ocean covers over half of the world! Kids will dive deep into these amazing ocean habitats with Elmo and his friends from Sesame Street"—Provided by publisher.
Identifiers: LCCN 2023006995 (print) | LCCN 2023006996 (ebook) | ISBN 9798765604267 (library binding) | ISBN 9798765617625 (epub)
Subjects: LCSH: Marine animals—Habitations—Juvenile literature. | Marine ecology—Juvenile literature. | BISAC: JUVENILE NONFICTION / Science & Nature / Environmental Science & Ecosystems
Classification: LCC QL122.2 .R4 2024 (print) | LCC QL122.2 (ebook) | DDC 591.77—dc23/eng/20230424

LC record available at https://lccn.loc.gov/2023006995
LC ebook record available at https://lccn.loc.gov/2023006996

ISBN 979-8-7656-2488-3 (pbk.)

Manufactured in the United States of America
1-1009563-51413-6/15/2023